This book is a presentation of Weekly Reader
Books. Weekly Reader Books offers book
clubs for children from preschool through high
school. For further information write to:
WEEKLY READER BOOKS, 4343 Equity Drive,
Columbus, Ohio 43228

This edition is published by arrangement
with Checkerboard Press.

Weekly Reader is a federally registered trademark
of Field Publications.

WEEKLY READER BOOKS presents

What Is a Desert?

A **Just Ask**™ Book

Hi, my name is Christopher!

by Chris Arvetis
and Carole Palmer

illustrated by
Jim Conahan

FIELD PUBLICATIONS
MIDDLETOWN, CT.

It's a desert.

A DESERT—
what's a desert?

First of all, you said it was
hot, and you're right.

No clouds are in the sky,
so the rays of the sun
are very strong.

The sun makes the desert
land very hot.

A desert is dry, too.
It does not rain often.
Some deserts go for years
without rain.
Then a heavy rainstorm
brings a lot of water
in a very short time.

We can use
the rain!

A desert is windy.
The sun heats the air and
causes the air to move.
The air moves so fast that
it becomes a strong wind.

The desert is covered with sand.
The wind blows the sand into hills
or ridges called sand dunes.

In some deserts, there are flat-topped mountains and smaller hills.

Interesting shapes!

Rainstorms make gulleys in the hills as the water runs down the steep slopes.
Soil washed down with the water forms fan-shaped ridges at the bottom.

Plants grow in the desert.
Do you know what these are?

Right, that's a cactus with
the bird peeking out.
From this palm tree
I can see sagebrush.

Mice, snakes, owls,
birds, scorpions,
and even turtles live
in the desert.

I know him!
Hi, Christopher!

Most of all—
remember a desert is hot.
It is dry and windy.
It has lots of sand.
And many special plants
and animals live there.